MW01049686

THE HOUSE ON MANGO STREET

by
Sandra Cisneros

Teacher Guide

Written by
Phyllis A. Green

Note

The Vintage Contemporaries paperback edition of the book was used to prepare this guide. The page references may differ in the hardcover or other paperback editions.

Please note: Please assess the appropriateness of this book for the age level and maturity of your students prior to reading and discussing it with your class.

ISBN 978-1-56137-483-0

To order, contact your local school supply store, or—

Novel Units, Inc.
P.O. Box 97
Bulverde, TX 78163-0097

Web site: www.novelunits.com

Table of Contents

Summary

Esperanza Cordero is growing up in the Hispanic quarter of Chicago. She shares her insights and maturing in 44 short vignettes about the people and places in her neighborhood. Her forthright disarming observations reveal not only Esperanza, but the realities of growing up in a poor urban setting.

About the Author

Sandra Cisneros was born in Chicago to a Mexican father and a Mexican-American mother in 1954. She grew up in the Wicker Park neighborhood of Chicago with six brothers. After she was graduated from Loyola University—Chicago with a degree in education, she was employed as a teacher to high school dropouts, a visiting poet, an arts administrator, and a college recruiter. Most recently, she has travelled across the country as a visiting professor of literature. She has been awarded two National Endowment for the Arts fellowships, a Lannon Foundation Literary Award, and a lecture appointment at the University of California—Berkeley. Ms. Cisneros currently lives in San Antonio, Texas. She is the author of *Woman Hollering Creek*, *Bad Boys*, and *My Wicked Wicked Ways* as well as *The House on Mango Street*. Her biography states that she is nobody's mother and nobody's wife.

Initiating Activities

1. Complete a K-W-L Chart, recording in the "K" column what students know of Mexican-American people and culture and the Hispanic section of Chicago. The "W" column is used for questions and expectations about the book (what you expect or anticipate learning by reading the book). The "L" column is reserved for use after reading the book to record what you've learned.

K	W	L

2. Listen to the first chapter of the book being read by Sandra Cisneros on the Random House audio-cassette. What do you learn about the teller of the story? Make some predictions about the book.

3. When was the book published? *(1989, 1984)* What was happening in Chicago at that time? in the world? among Mexican-American early teen-age girls? Investigate and then make some predictions.

4. Look at the book's dedication. *(A las Mujeres, To the Women)* Why does an author dedicate a book? What does this particular dedication suggest to you about the book?

5. Collect clues from the book to make predictions. Look at pictures on the cover. Read the quoted reviews. Thumb through the book. What does the style of print on the cover and chapter titles suggest to you?

Organization of the Guide

Vocabulary words are identified and Discussion Questions are included chapter-by-chapter. After each eight chapters, Supplementary Activity suggestions are listed. Initiating Activities and Culminating Activities are provided also.

Because of the vignette nature of the book, it is suggested that students could, gradually as the book is read, develop on-going images and graphic representations. Here are some suggestions:

1. A photo collage (see page 6 of this guide).

2. A class or small group mural featuring places and people from the book.

3. A Readers' Theatre presentation with the students speaking as the various characters from the book.

4. A sound recording of various non-word impressions.

5. A chart of the various characters.

Character	One-Word Summary	Most Prominent Physical Feature	Identification: Age, Sex, Occupation, Heritage	Do You Know Anyone Similar?

6. A map of the places on Mango Street.

7. As an ensemble cast, who would you choose to play the various parts in a play created from the book? Keep adding to your cast as you read on. Feel free to revise your cast members as you read further.

Vocabulary Activities

Overview: Vocabulary challenge words are identified chapter-by-chapter. It is suggested that a portion of each day's reading instructional time be spent in vocabulary-building. Here are some suggested activities:

1. Play word games such as Memory, Scrabble, Boggle. Provide bonus points for using vocabulary challenge words.

2. Construct matrix puzzles for classmates to solve. For example:

Category	Features			
	Strong	Poor	American	Hispanic
Houses	Log Cabin			
Streets	Expressway			
Books	Dictionary			
Games	Wrestling			

3. Collect Spanish words on a chart or graphic. Use pictures to identify the meaning.

4. Create word maps for selected vocabulary challenge words according to their part of speech. (See pages 7-9 of this guide for examples.)

5. Collect at least one new word each day. Devise your own way to remember your words (3 x 5 cards, a vocabulary listing in the manner of a memo pad, listing on a post-it) and review your words daily until they are truly remembered.

A Photo Collage for *The House on Mango Street*

Directions: In each of the mat holes, illustrate one or a group of the important people and places in the book. Include identification sentences in the manner of a photo collage.

Word Map for a Noun

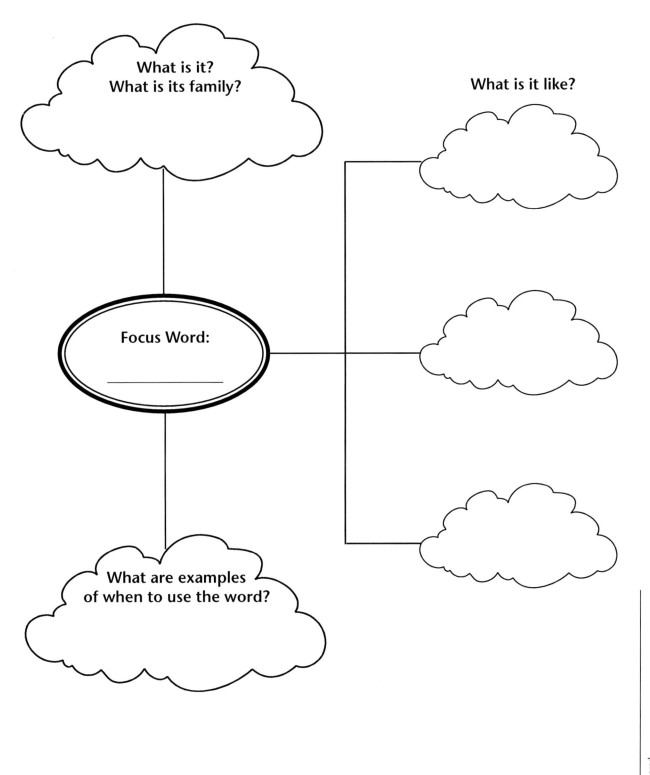

What is it?
What is its family?

What is it like?

Focus Word:

_____

What are examples
of when to use the word?

Word Map for a Verb

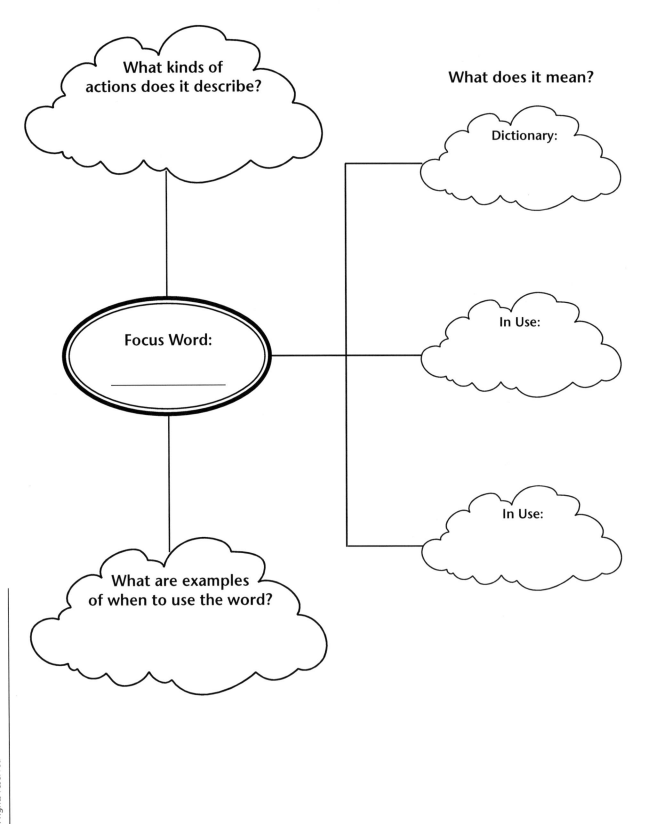

What kinds of
actions does it describe?

What does it mean?

Dictionary:

Focus Word:

_____

In Use:

In Use:

What are examples
of when to use the word?

Word Map for an Adjective

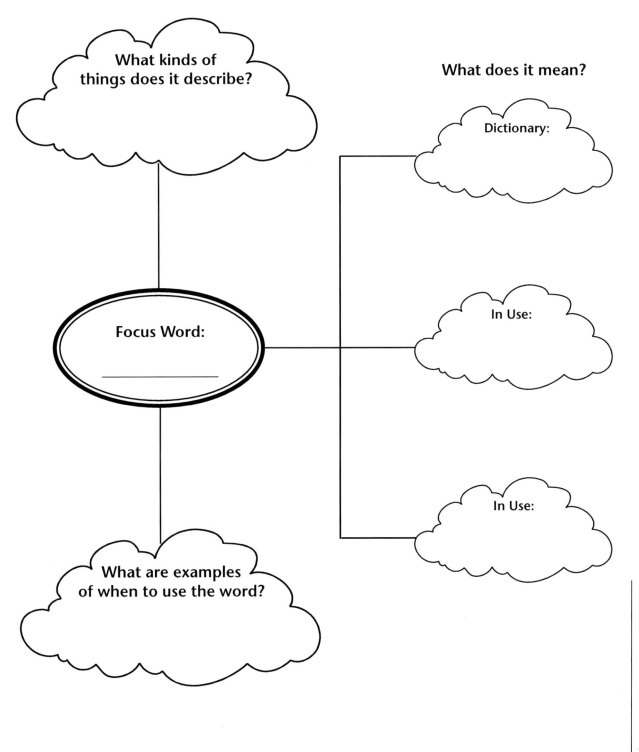

What kinds of
things does it describe?

What does it mean?

Dictionary:

Focus Word:

_____

In Use:

In Use:

What are examples
of when to use the word?

Using Predictions

We all make predictions as we read—little guesses about what will happen next, how the conflict will be resolved, which details given by the author will be important to the plot, which details will help to fill in our sense of a character. Students should be encouraged to predict, to make sensible guesses. As students work on predictions, these discussion questions can be used to guide them: What are some of the ways to predict? What is the process of a sophisticated reader's thinking and predicting? What clues does an author give us to help us in making our predictions? Why are some predictions more likely than others?

A predicting chart is for students to record their predictions. As each subsequent chapter is discussed, you can review and correct previous predictions. This procedure serves to focus on predictions and to review the stories.

Use the facts and ideas the author gives.

Use your own knowledge.

Use new information that may cause you to change your mind.

Predictions:

_____

_____

_____

_____

Prediction Chart

What characters have we met so far?	What is the conflict in the story?	What are your predictions?	Why did you make those predictions?

Story Map

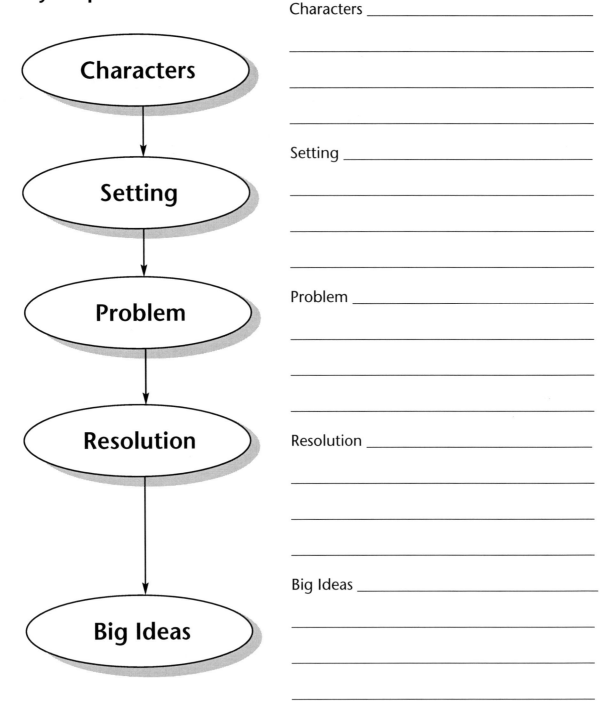

Characters _____

_____

_____

_____

Setting _____

_____

_____

_____

Problem _____

_____

_____

_____

Resolution _____

_____

_____

_____

Big Ideas _____

_____

_____

_____

Using Character Webs

Attribute Webs are simply a visual representation of a character from the novel. They provide a systematic way for the students to organize and recap the information they have about a particular character. Attribute webs may be used after reading the novel to recapitulate information about a particular character or completed gradually as information unfolds, done individually, or finished as a group project.

One type of character attribute web uses these divisions:

• How a character acts and feels. (How does the character feel in this picture? How would you feel if this happened to you? How do you think the character feels?)

• How a character looks. (Close your eyes and picture the character. Describe him to me.)

• Where a character lives. (Where and when does the character live?)

• How others feel about the character. (How does another specific character feel about our character?)

In group discussion about the student attribute webs and specific characters, the teacher can ask for backup proof from the novel. You can also include inferential thinking.

Attribute webs need not be confined to characters. They may also be used to organize information about a concept, object or place.

Attribute Web

The attribute web below is designed to help you gather clues the author provides about what a character is like. Fill in the blanks with words and phrases which tell how the character acts and looks, as well as what the character says and what others say about him or her.

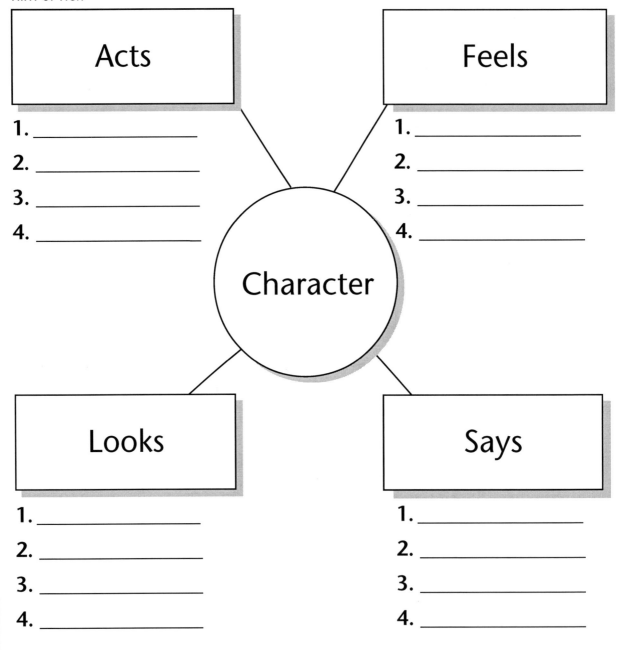

Attribute Web

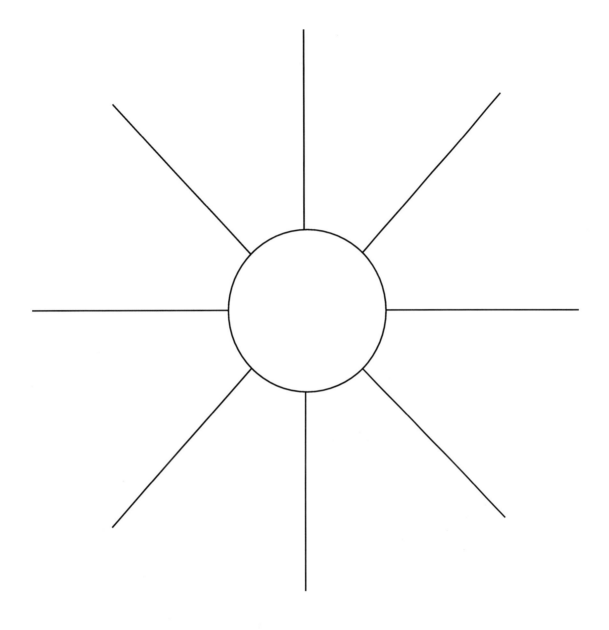

"The House on Mango Street"—Pages 3-5

Vocabulary:

boarded 4   temporary 5

Discussion Questions and Activities:

1. Who tells the story? *(The reader isn't sure yet, but you do know it is a child. Sibling names suggest Hispanic heritage.)*

2. How does it feel to move? *(Answers vary.)* How does the storyteller feel about moving? *(impatient, sad, unhappy, dissatisfied)*

3. Draw a picture of the house on Mango Street, using the author's word pictures to guide you.

"Hairs"—Pages 6-7

Vocabulary:

barrettes 6   rosettes 6

Discussion Questions and Activities:

1. Why does the storyteller tell about her family members' hair? *(to help identify them, to establish an informal childlike manner)*

2. What is "hair that smells like bread"? *(Mama's hair and the feeling of safety and security that Mama brings.)*

"Boys and Girls"—Pages 8-9

Vocabulary:

universe 8   responsibility 8   anchor 9

Discussion Questions and Activities:

1. Is the storyteller really a balloon as she says on page 9? *(No, it is a literary device called a metaphor, a comparison without using "like" or "as.")* Why is the balloon tied to an anchor a good description? *(The girl could fly away as a happy joyful red balloon, but she is held back by her responsibility for her sister.)*

2. Why don't Carlos and Kiki watch out for Nenny? *(The author suggests that these older brothers aren't expected to have responsibility for their younger sisters.)* Have you heard of such differentiation between expectations for boys and girls? Share your experiences with a classmate.

"My Name"—Pages 10-11

Vocabulary:

chandelier 11   inherited 11

Discussion Questions and Activities:

1. What is Esperanza's attitude toward her name? *(She understands the family heritage of her name, but she wishes she could have a different name. She does understand the difference in the sound of Esperanza in Spanish and when spoken by non-Spanish speaking people.)*

2. How do most children feel about their names? *(Answers vary.)* Write a few paragraphs to tell about your own name and how you feel about it.

3. Explain the statement, "but I think this is a Chinese lie because the Chinese, like the Mexicans, don't like their women strong."

"Cathy Queen of Cats"—Pages 12-13

Vocabulary:

raggedy 12

Discussion Questions and Activities:

1. What is distinctive about Cathy? *(She has many, many cats at her house.)*

2. What does the neighborhood getting bad mean? *(Answers vary. The neighborhood residents are changing.)*

3. Do you think Cathy's father will fly to France one day? Give reasons for your opinion.

"Our Good Day"—Pages 14-16

Vocabulary:

chip 14

Discussion Questions and Activities:

1. Who are Lucy and Rachel? *(Two sisters who live on Mango Street and buy a bicycle with Esperanza.)*

2. How does Cathy react to Lucy and Rachel? *(She doesn't like them and avoids them.)* How does she reach her opinion? *(by evaluating Lucy and Rachel's shabby appearance)* How is Cathy's reasoning flawed?

"Laughter"—Pages 17-18

Discussion Questions and Activities:
1. How do Nenny and Esperanza laugh? *(robust and spontaneous)* How does the author tell you? *(by using a simile "all of a sudden and surprised like a pile of dishes breaking")*

2. How old is Esperanza? Give reasons from the book for your answers.

"Gil's Furniture Bought & Sold"—Pages 19-20

Vocabulary:
marimbas 20

Discussion Questions and Activities:
1. Draw a picture of Gil's Furniture Store, each student adding to the picture drawn with chalk on the chalkboard.

2. Why does Esperanza find the music box so fascinating? *(It's unique and new to her.)* What makes something fascinating to you?

Supplementary Activities:
1. Start a simile collection. Cisneros writes with many similes. In a collage format, draw pictures of the images she uses. Other students can try to match with what she is describing. See pages 22-23 of this guide for a simile collection reproducible master.

2. Start an attribute web for Esperanza. (See pages 13-15 of this guide.)

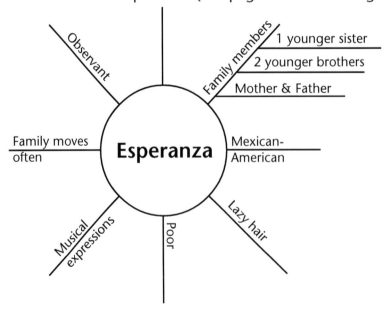

3. Devise a map of the neighborhood.

4. Compare a store you know well to Gil's Furniture Store.

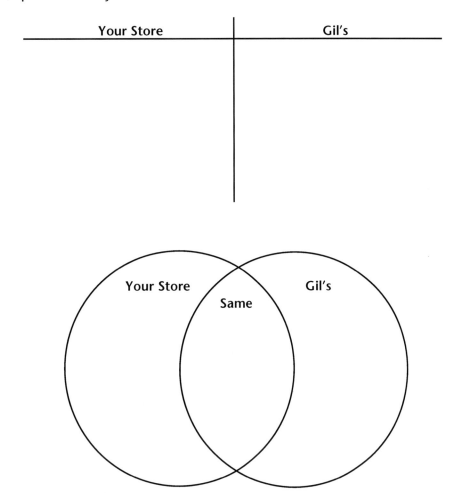

Your Store	Gil's

5. Analysis: Why does the author use informal language? incomplete sentences?

6. Collect interesting names for a name splash. Put the names on 3 x 5 cards to sort and categorize later.

7. Listen to some Mexican music to get a feeling of the book's setting.

Similes and Metaphors

page 6, "hair is like a broom"

page 6, "hair like fur"

page 6, "hair, like little rosettes"

page 6, "hair...like little candy circles"

page 9, "red balloon... tied to an anchor"

page 17, "the shy ice cream bells giggle"

page 17, "laughter...all of a sudden and surprised like a pile of dishes breaking"

page 22, "steps...jutting like crooked teeth"

page 25, "nose...Cadillac was all pleated like an alligator's"

page 29, "kids...almost break like fancy museum vases you can't replace"

page 30, "Angel Vargas...dropped from the sky like a sugar donut"

page 39, "feet...like thick tamales"

page 39, "feet were lovely as pink pearls"

pages 39-40, "toes, pale and see-through like a salamander's"

page 40, "feet... descended like white pigeons"

page 49, "you...waiting like a new Buick with the keys in the ignition"

page 50, "[hips] as wide as a boat"

page 70, "[smell] like books that have been left out in the rain"

page 71, "dogs...leap and somersault like an apostrophe and comma"

page 71, "[complexion] like salamanders that have never seen the sun"

page 73, "toenails like little pink seashells"

page 73, "[emotions] waiting to explode like Christmas"

page 75, "droop like tulips in a glass"

page 81, "eyes like Egypt"

page 81, "black like raven feathers"

page 81, "flicks her hair back like a satin shawl"

page 84, "pieces of paper that smell like a dime"

page 84, "sad like a house on fire"

page 90, "lungs powerful as morning glories"

page 95, "weeds like so many squinty-eyed stars"

page 103, "laughter like tin"

page 103, "hands like porcelain"

page 105, "smelled like cinnamon"

See if you can find additional similes or metaphors:

Simile Collecting

Directions: Identify these items which figure in similes in the book. Use the page number of the simile in the book.

,

,

"Meme Ortiz"—Pages 21-22

Vocabulary:

>   lopsided 22   gutters 22

Discussion Questions and Activities:
1. How do you know in this chapter that the storyteller is a child? *(She emphasizes the child who lives in each of the houses she includes as well as the activities of children.)*

2. Is there any humor in the chapter? in the story? *(Answers vary. The descriptions are often funny as are the short sudden explanations as the last sentence in the chapter.)*

3. Why would someone give a different name when being introduced?

"Louie, His Cousin & His Other Cousin"—Pages 23-25

Vocabulary:

>   automatically 24   sirens 24   flooring 24

Discussion Questions and Activities:
1. Describe Louie's cousins. *(Marin wore dark hose, lots of make-up, sold Avon, baby-sat with Louie's sisters, and sang from the doorway of the basement apartment. Louie's other cousin came by in a big yellow Cadillac.)*

2. Why was Louie's cousin put in handcuffs? *(He had stolen the yellow Cadillac or so the police believed.)*

3. Why does the author give more detail about Marin? *(The child observes Marin more.)*

"Marin"—Pages 26-27

Discussion Questions and Activities:
1. Why is Marin living with Louie's family? *(Her family in Puerto Rico has sent her to the U. S. to visit relatives. The full reason isn't known.)*

2. Explain this phrase: "Is waiting for a car to stop, a star to fall, someone to change her life." *(Marin wishes for something exciting to happen to her, but she doesn't do anything to make things happen herself.)* Do you favor this approach to life? What is the author's attitude?

"Those Who Don't"—Page 28

Discussion Questions and Activities:
1. Why do outsiders feel afraid on Mango Street? *(They don't know about the people and safety. They are ignorant of the neighborhood.)*

2. What does, "All brown all around, we are safe" mean? *(The Mexican and Hispanics on Mango Street are all brown-skinned. They feel safe living together, but would be fearful in a different neighborhood.)*

3. Do you agree with the sentiments expressed in this chapter? Why or why not?

"There Was an Old Woman She Had So Many Children She Didn't Know What to Do"—Pages 29-30

Discussion Questions and Activities:
1. What was Rosa Vargas' fate? *(She had a large family. Her man left without a word or any money to help.)*

2. How does the author emphasize Rosa's daily routine with alliteration? *(On page 29 she uses a lot of "b" words—buttoning, bottling, and babying. Then the description of the kids includes "bend trees and bounce between cars.")*

3. Notice how Cisneros ends the chapter. *(Angel Vargas dropped from the sky and exploded down to earth.)* Look back over other chapters to look for similar chapter endings.

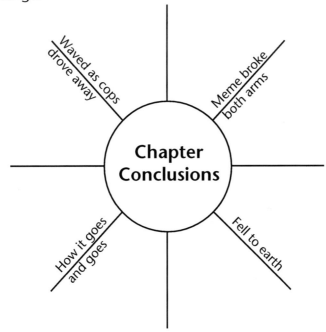

What general statements can you make about the chapter endings? Is the technique effective?

"Alicia Who Sees Mice"—Pages 31-32

Vocabulary:
> tortilla 31

Discussion Questions and Activities:
1. What are Alicia's dreams and goals for herself? *(to go beyond the life her mother had)*

2. Why does Alicia bother with the tortilla star? *(Though dreaming of and working toward something different for herself, she still meets the traditional expectations for her role and that includes making the lunchbox tortillas.)*

3. What is Alicia afraid of? *(mice and fathers)* Why?

"Darius & the Clouds"—Pages 33-34

Discussion Questions and Activities:
1. "You can never have too much sky." What does the statement mean? Is it true?

2. How is Darius in contrast to the clouds he describes? *(Darius is sometimes stupid and sometimes a fool, but he speaks of a universal God.)*

"And Some More"—Pages 35-38

Vocabulary:
> cumulus 36   nimbus 36   frijoles 37

Discussion Questions and Activities:
1. Why are there so many indentations (paragraphs) in this chapter? *(different speakers naming themselves)* What about no quotation marks? *(Answers vary. This book uses an informal style.)*

2. Using all the class, read the chapter aloud with different students taking different parts. How can you, in this oral reading, create the scene Cisneros describes? *(Answers vary. Speak lyrically and conversationally. Use voices and accents likely to be heard on Mango Street.)*

Supplementary Activities:
1. How do neighborhoods vary? What creates or constitutes a neighborhood? What do neighborhoods have in common? How big is a neighborhood?

Describe your own neighborhood. Use a narrative paragraph or graphic organizer (attribute web or chart or design one of your own) or an illustration to represent your neighborhood.

2. Use the letters in neighborhood to summarize Esperanza's neighborhood. Use a word or phrase starting with each of the letters of the word.

N _____

E _____

I _____

G _____

H _____

B _____

O _____

R _____

H _____

O _____

O _____

D _____

3. What is "a woman's place"? How do different people and cultures vary in their definitions? Interview parents and grandparents to expand your ideas on this question.

4. Create a cloud-naming bulletin board. On a blue background, place your own particular named cloud. Explain your depiction.

5. Generate a class name book. Each class member contributes a page telling about his own name. Investigate the etymology of the name, tell any special family significance, and tell how you react to the name personally.

"The Family of Little Feet"—Pages 39-42

Vocabulary:

doughy 39	tamales 39	salamander's 40
strutting 41	stoop 41	

Discussion Questions and Activities:
1. What does Esperanza's naming of her neighbors tell you about her? *(Answers vary. She names people in a childish, single characteristic descriptive way.)*

2. What adventures happened because of the lemon, red, and pale blue shoes? *(The girls tried on the shoes and strutted down the block.)*

3. What do you think of the bum man? *(He's rude and unpleasant and children should avoid him.)*

4. Explain the last sentence of the chapter. *(The girls don't care about the shoes because they are reminders of the nasty bum man.)*

"A Rice Sandwich"—Pages 43-45

Vocabulary:

canteen 43	Spartan 44	anemic 44
appreciate 44	hollered 44	boulevard 45

Discussion Questions and Activities:
1. Who are the special kids? *(The ones who wear keys around their necks—the latchkey children whose parents aren't home during the day.)*

2. Why does Esperanza want to stay at school and eat lunch in the canteen? *(She's curious and thinks it might be fun.)*

3. How does she convince her mother to let her stay for lunch? *(She wears her down with asking and pleading.)* How would you convince your mother of something similar?

4. How does staying for lunch work out for Esperanza? *(Badly—the canteen nun requires approval of the principal who is only agreeable for one day because she feels sorry for Esperanza. The canteen is nothing special. Her rice sandwich is cold and the bread is greasy.)*

"Chanclas"—Pages 46-48

Vocabulary:

chanclas 46   tamales 47

Discussion Questions and Activities:

1. Explain the title of the chapter. *(Chanclas are old shoes or sandals. Esperanza in this chapter is ashamed of her shoes.)*

2. Is Esperanza justified in being so concerned about her shoes?

3. Notice how the author makes the scene vivid with details about the setting. Look for examples in this chapter. *(little rose on the new slip, feet scuffed and round with heels all crooked, brown gum stuck beneath the sea, chair stamped Precious Blood, linoleum floor)*

"Hips"—Pages 49-52

Vocabulary:

authority 50   merengue 51   tembleque 51
naphtha 52   disgusted 52

Discussion Questions and Activities:

1. Why does the author have a chapter on hips? *(The 12-year-old girls in the book are concerned about maturing physically and hips are one of the physical signs.)*

2. In small cooperative groups, create a collage about hips. Using pictures torn from magazines, assemble a collage to depict what is said in this chapter.

3. At recess or during gym class, use a jump rope to reenact the girls' game from the chapter.

"The First Job"—Pages 53-55

Vocabulary:

hydrant 53   bus fare 54   negatives 54

Discussion Questions and Activities:

1. What is Esperanza's first job? *(matching negatives with their prints)* What are the pluses and minuses to the job?

+	-
•Makes money	•Boring, repetitive
•Didn't have to look hard for the job	•Strange, unfamiliar
	•Older Oriental man

2. How are the girls in the book treated by the men they meet? *(forward, badly, disrespectfully)*

"Papa Who Wakes Up Tired in the Dark"—Pages 56-57

Vocabulary:

abuelito 56　　　　　Está muerto 56　　　　　crumples 56

Discussion Questions and Activities:

1. Why is this a sad chapter? *(Esperanza's grandmother has died and her Papa cries.)*

2. What kind of life does Esperanza's Papa have? *(hard, works long hours at labor intensive job)*

3. How does Esperanza grow up in this chapter? *(She takes her responsibility as the oldest child and she understands her father's sadness.)*

"Born Bad"—Pages 58-61

Vocabulary:

limp 58　　　　　imitate 59

Discussion Questions and Activities:

1. Why does Esperanza feel guilty about Aunt Lupe? *(She and her friends imitated Aunt Lupe in her weakened sickly state and then Aunt Lupe died.)*

2. How does Esperanza explain diseases? *(Random arbitrary choice of the unlucky one to get sick with no reason as to who gets stricken.)*

3. Do you agree with Esperanza's explanation of diseases? Why or why not? Consider the statement that Esperanza's explanation may be as good as any because <u>we don't know</u> what causes many illnesses.

4. What was special about Aunt Lupe? *(She enjoyed Esperanza's poetry and encouraged her to keep writing.)*

5. What does the following statement mean: "You must keep writing. It will keep you free"? *(Answers vary. Keeps your mind and spirit free. Provides a creative outlet. Gives you something special beyond whatever unpleasantness your daily life may have.)*

"Elenita, Cards, Palm, Water"—Pages 62-64

Vocabulary:

voodoo 63   los espíritus 63   pillar 63

Discussion Questions and Activities:
1. What does the chapter describe? *(Esperanza having her fortune told.)*

2. What is Esperanza's attitude toward the fortune-telling? Give as many answers as you can. *(disappointment, skeptical, hopeful, expectant)*

3. Cite instances of superstitions in the book. *(page 64)* Start a class list of superstitions you've heard. Choose one to describe when and where you've heard it.

4. What is a "home in the heart" and why is it disappointing? *(It is a dream, a thought, and isn't real.)*

Supplementary Activities:
1. What are Esperanza's dreams for the future? Compare her dreams to the dreams of adolescents you know.

Esperanza	Other Adolescents

2. What realities does Esperanza discover in the book? Discuss in small groups. Consider class, gender, racial dislike, sexuality.

3. Consider your father or another adult man you know. Look back to the title of the chapter starting on page 56. Represent your father or another adult in similar phrasing.

4. Interview older siblings and parents about their first jobs. What similarities do you find to Esperanza's first job?

"Geraldo No Last Name"—Pages 65-66

Vocabulary:

cumbias 65	salsas 65	rancheras 65
brazer 66	wetback 66	currency exchange 66

Discussion Questions and Activities:
1. What happened to Geraldo? *(He died after a hit-and-run accident.)*

2. Why was the surgeon so late in coming to work on Geraldo? *(Answers vary.)*

3. How are people identified? How was Geraldo identified? *(by superficial things—his shirt color)*

4. What is the author's feeling about Geraldo? *(sad, indignant, resigned)*

"Edna's Ruthie"—Pages 67-69

Vocabulary:
babushka 67

Discussion Questions and Activities:
1. What is strange about Ruthie? *(She can't make decisions and lives on Mango Street and sleeps on her mother's couch though she says she has a real house all her own.)*

2. How can you explain Ruthie? *(She lies or is mistaken about her alternatives.)*

3. Have you ever met anyone like Ruthie? in a book? in this book? Compare Ruthie to Cathy Queen of Cats. *(pages 12-13)*

"The Earl of Tennessee"—Pages 70-71

Vocabulary:

somersault 71	crook 71

Discussion Questions and Activities:
1. Why would someone be named the Earl of Tennessee? *(Answers vary—a child's name, to associate with a song, to be important.)*

2. Why is Earl a mystery to the neighborhood children? *(He never really interacts with them. The children just observe him. His wife is a mystery, too.)*

3. Have you encountered a neighborhood mystery person? How did you react? Did you invent details? Share a story of such a person. Be sure to use fake names.

"Sire"—Pages 72-73

Discussion Questions and Activities:
1. What do the questions in this chapter suggest about Esperanza's thinking? *(She is growing up and wondering about boyfriends.)*

2. How is Lois a paradox, a contradiction? *(She acts like an adult, but is small and can't tie her shoes.)*

3. Are there other paradoxes, contradictions, in the book?

"Four Skinny Trees"—Pages 74-75

Vocabulary:

raggedy 74	appreciate 74	ferocious 74
despite 75		

Discussion Questions and Activities:
1. What do the four skinny trees remind Esperanza of? *(herself)*

2. Using a T-diagram, compare Esperanza and the city trees.

	City Trees	Esperanza
Appearance:	•Tall and skinny •Raggedy	•Pointy elbows •Shabby
Strength:	•Secret •Roots	•Secret •Anger
Challenge:	•Survival	•Survival, thriving in a difficult environment

Is the comparison appropriate? Have you ever read before of a person compared to a tree?

"No Speak English"—Pages 76-78

Vocabulary:

Mamasota 76	fuchsia roses 76	lavender 77
hamandeggs 77	hollyhocks 77	hysterical 78

Discussion Questions and Activities:

1. What is the color for this chapter? *(pink)* Why is it appropriate? *(Mamacita is a subservient female and pink is traditionally the color for girls.)*

2. What three characteristics most define Mamacita? *(Her large size, her love of pink, and her inability to speak English.)*

3. What does the author feel about Mamacita? *(Sorry, pities her, but shows her as unable or unwilling to change her fate.)*

4. What does "Mamasota" mean?

"Rafaela Who Drinks Coconut & Papaya Juice on Tuesdays"—Pages 79-80

Vocabulary:

papaya 80

Discussion Questions and Activities:

1. What is the situation of the women on Mango Street? (See graphic on page 35 of this guide.)

2. Can you make any general statements about how the author feels about the women who live on Mango Street? Discuss the question with a partner and then contribute to a class word map answer.

"Sally"—Pages 81-83

Discussion Questions and Activities:

1. What is Sally's "problem"? *(She is too beautiful and so her father is **very** protective.)* Is it strange to call beauty a problem? Why?

2. Esperanza imagines what Sally might wish for in contrast to her Mango Street existence. Where do these ideas originate? Are they realistic ideas?

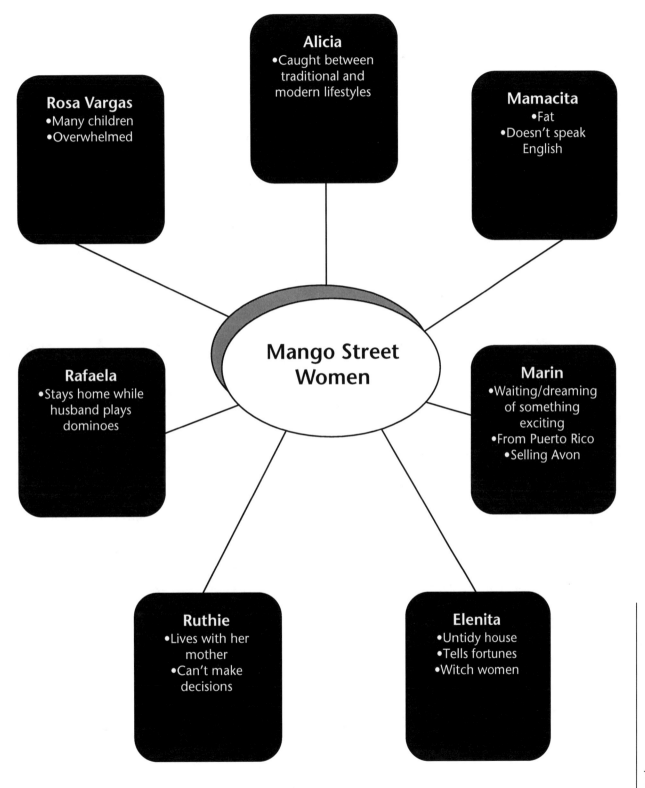

Rosa Vargas
•Many children
•Overwhelmed

Alicia
•Caught between traditional and modern lifestyles

Mamacita
•Fat
•Doesn't speak English

Mango Street Women

Rafaela
•Stays home while husband plays dominoes

Marin
•Waiting/dreaming of something exciting
•From Puerto Rico
•Selling Avon

Ruthie
•Lives with her mother
•Can't make decisions

Elenita
•Untidy house
•Tells fortunes
•Witch women

Supplementary Activities:
1. What is the organization of this book? First think about what other books it reminds you of. What pictures come to mind as you think of this book? What is the emphasis (message, theme) of the book? Do any of the chapters cluster about general themes or pictures? In small groups, start to prepare original story maps to summarize the book.

2. Return to the predictions you made before reading the book. Which ideas have proved correct? Revise your predictions.

3. Compare your neighborhood to Mango Street.

4. Using the graphic on page 37, place the people in the book in houses.

5. Using a magazine, choose pictures of houses each of five chosen characters from the book would enjoy.

6. Start a list of nice pleasant things about Mango Street.

"Minerva Writes Poems"—Pages 84-85

Discussion Questions and Activities:
1. What does a dime smell like? *(Answers vary.)* How do you react to the many similes in the book? Do the similes make the word pictures more real? How do the similes suggest the age and viewpoint of the book's narrator?

2. Is Minerva a victim? Why? What options does she have?

"Bums in the Attic"—Pages 86-87

Discussion Questions and Activities:
1. Is Esperanza justified in saying she is ashamed on Sunday outings? Why or why not.

2. Explain the chapter's title. *(Esperanza dreams about having her own house and inviting bums to live in the attic.)*

"Beautiful & Cruel"—Pages 88-89

Vocabulary:
threshold 88

Discussion Questions and Activities:
1. Esperanza has decided not to grow up tame. What does that mean?

Houses on Mango Street

2. What is Esperanza's developing opinion of men? Think back over the men she's described in the book. Collect your ideas about these men and then write a short paragraph to answer the question.

3. Why do the chapter titles have ampersands instead of "and" written out?

"A Smart Cookie"—Pages 90-91

Vocabulary:
comadres 91

Discussion Questions and Activities:
1. How is Esperanza different from her mother? How does she resemble her mother?

2. What advice would her mother give Esperanza? *(Don't be ashamed.)*

3. Point out the irony in this chapter. *(Esperanza's mother became a smart cookie after she made some bad choices.)*

4. How does this saying relate to the chapter, "Good judgment comes from experience. Experience comes from bad judgment"?

"What Sally Said"—Pages 92-93

Vocabulary:
sweetbread 93

Discussion Questions and Activities:
1. Why does the author use such an unvarnished, straight-forward telling of child abuse? *(It suggests the child of Esperanza honestly relating the story. It makes the fact of child abuse more appalling.)*

2. Why did Sally go home with her father from Esperanza's house? *(Answers vary.)*

"The Monkey Garden"—Pages 94-98

Vocabulary:

twangy 94	cockscombs 94	hibiscus 95
unicorn 96		

Discussion Questions and Activities:
1. Describe the monkey garden when it was pretty. *(pages 94-95)*

2. How did the monkey garden start to decay? *(No one was tending the garden and abandoned cars and other debris began being left in the garden.)*

3. How did Sally's comment on page 96, "Play with the kids if you want...I'm staying here" tell about her changes? *(She is acting more adolescent. She's more interested in the teen-age boys than she is in the garden.)*

4. Why did Esperanza develop a headache? *(She was embarrassed and appalled at Sally's actions. She said she wanted to be dead.)*

5. What did Esperanza learn from the incidents in this chapter? *(The garden had lost its appeal because she didn't like the lessons she'd learned about men and women, boys and girls, and her friend Sally.)*

"Red Clowns"—Pages 99-100

Discussion Questions and Activities:

1. What did Sally lie about? *(The way teen-age boys treat teen-age girls.)*

2. How can you describe the mood in the "Red Clowns" chapter? Look for one or two words. *(lament, sad, outraged)*

3. Explain the "Red Clowns" title. *(The title is ironic because the events of the chapter are sad as contrasted to the happy laughing red clowns image.)*

4. Why don't the teen-age boys call Esperanza by name? *(They don't care about her as a person, only as a female.)*

"Linoleum Roses"—Pages 101-102

Discussion Questions and Activities:

1. What is Sally's fate? *(marries a marshmallow salesman, going to another state to get married because of her young age)*

2. What kind of contrasts does the author create in this chapter? *(Sally marries to escape, but actually is still not free.)* How many times are "except" and "but" used in the chapter? *(four times)*

3. Detail the chapter's contrasts.

Sally is young and not ready, ———————————→ but married.

Sally says she is in love, ———————————→ but Esperanza thinks she did it to escape.

She buys her own things ———————————→ when her husband gives her money.

She is happy, ———————————→ except sometimes her husband gets angry.

Most days her husband is okay, ———————————→ except he won't let her talk on the telephone or look out the window.

4. How does the author feel about Sally's husband? *(unimpressed and very irritated)* How do you know? *(The author leaves him without a name, gives him a funny occupation, and relates nothing positive about him.)*

Supplementary Activities:
1. What advice would you give to Sally?

2. Compare Sally and Esperanza.

	Sally	Esperanza
Home:		
Family:		
Abilities:		
Expectations:		

3. Choose a maxim to summarize the author's message to adolescent girls.

4. How does this book deal with stereotypes? Are there any stereotypical actions and people seen on the pages of the book? How should the reader deal with these stereotypes.

5. How do adolescents learn the expected adult roles they will assume? Brainstorm some answers for a web.

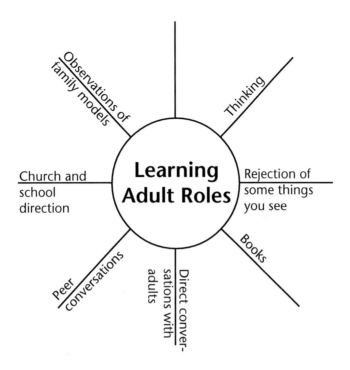

6. What is the author's attitude toward men? How do you know?

"The Three Sisters"—Pages 103-105

Vocabulary:

las comadres 103

Discussion Questions and Activities:

1. Did one of the sisters really have cat eyes? Who had marble hands? *(one of the sisters)* Would you advise an aspiring writer to use figurative language in this way? Give reasons for your answer.

2. Complete a figurative language web.

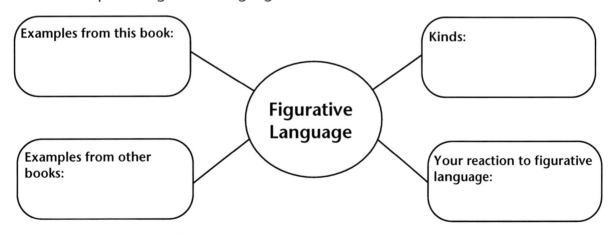

3. Explain the sisters. What is their "power"? Why do they give Esperanza advice? *(The sisters can read other people's minds—or so they believe. They sense or guess that Esperanza will go far from Mango Street.)*

4. True or false—"You can't erase what you know. You can't forget who you are."

"Alicia & I Talking on Edna's Steps"—Pages 106-107

Vocabulary:
  Guadalajara 106

Discussion Questions and Activities:
1. Why does Esperanza have a sadness? *(She doesn't think she has a house because she's ashamed of the house at 4006 Mango Street.)*

2. What is Esperanza's opinion of the mayor? *(The mayor doesn't care about Mango Street.)*

"A House of My Own"—Page 108

Discussion Questions and Activities:
1. How does Esperanza define a house of her own? *(ownership, appearance, by what it isn't)*

2. Notice how Cisneros often uses repetition in her writing. How is it an effective technique?

3. Describe a house of your own. Try using Cisneros' repetition technique.

"Mango Says Goodbye Sometimes"—Pages 109-110

Vocabulary:
  trudged 109

Discussion Questions and Activities:
1. What is the mood at the end of the book? *(Sad and depressing as to the neighbors and living situation on Mango Street, but also hopeful because Esperanza is sure she'll be leaving.)*

Culminating Activities

1. Complete the story map chart to summarize the book. (See page 12 of this guide.)

2. Choose your favorite neighborhood person. Share your choice and rationale for it by:

   • Preparing a written explanation.

   • Creating a collage or illustration presenting a monologue as that neighborhood person.

   • Explaining why that character represents for you the author's message in the book.

3. Describe Esperanza as she would be five years after the end of the book.

4. Prepare advice for Esperanza and/or her parents.

5. Design a Mango Street Museum.

6. Describe a Mango Street Reunion ten, twenty, thirty, or forty years later.

7. Select a favorite image from the book. Choose a painting or poem to remind you of that image. Explain your choices.

8. Celebrate your learning by doing one of the following:

   • Creating a board game of the story.

   • Creating a rap about the people who live on Mango Street.

   • Completing the final K-W-L column. (See page 3 of this guide.)

   • Choosing a favorite chapter to read to a parent or other adult for reaction.

   • Filling in literal and figurative webs about the Mango Street house. (See page 44 of this guide.)

   • Explaining the title and how the house is a symbol.

9. Summarize Cisneros' writing. Deal with these possible descriptions: feminist, lyrical, disarming, confrontive.

Literal Web

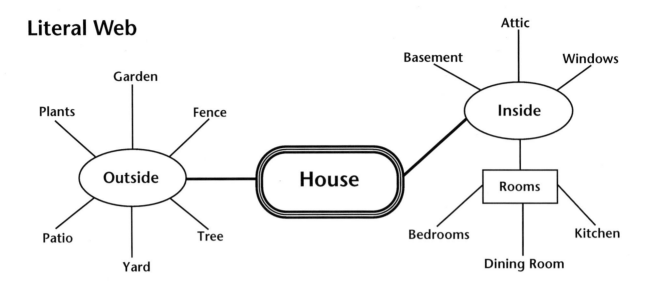

Figurative Web

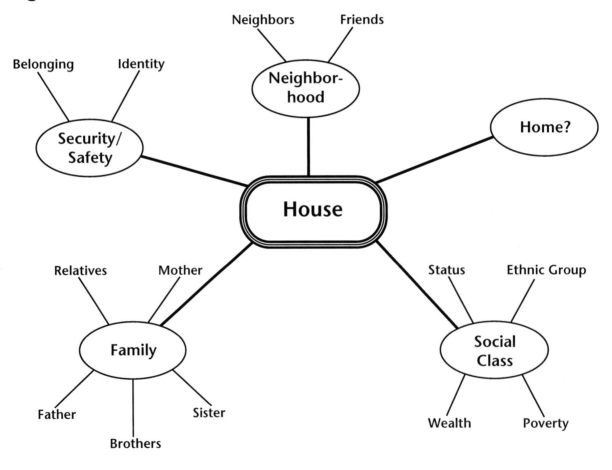